LIFE OF PI
MUSIC FROM THE MOTION PICTURE SOUNDTRACK

ISBN 978-1-4803-2132-8

HAL•LEONARD® CORPORATION
7777 W. BLUEMOUND RD. P.O. BOX 13819 MILWAUKEE, WI 53213

In Australia Contact:
Hal Leonard Australia Pty. Ltd.
4 Lentara Court
Cheltenham, Victoria, 3192 Australia
Email: ausadmin@halleonard.com.au

Visit Hal Leonard Online at
www.halleonard.com

3302885258

C000057608

PI'S LULLABY

Written by MYCHAEL DANNA
and BOMBAY JAYASHRI

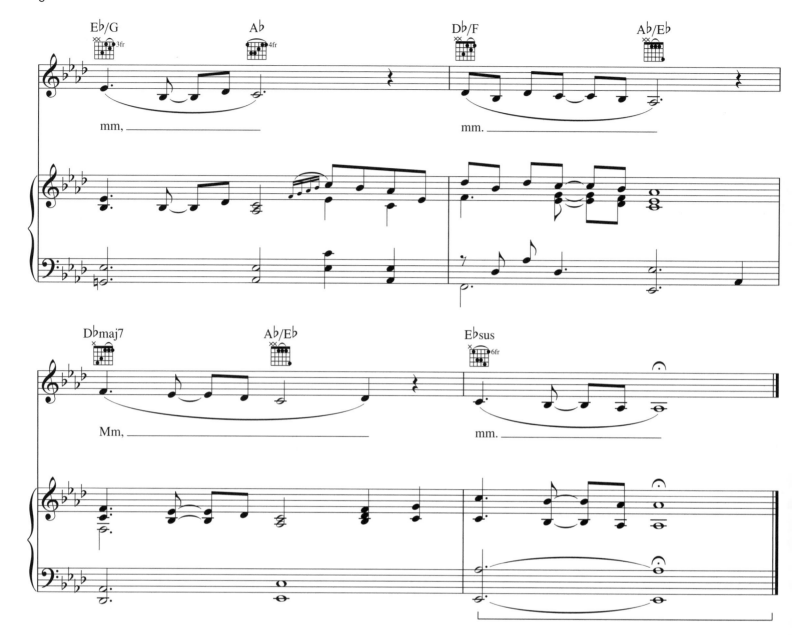

English Translation

Oh, my love,
Oh, the delight of my eyes,
Would you not sleep, my love?

Are you the plumage of the peacock?
Are you the cuckoo or the cry of the cuckoo?
Are you the moon or the light of the moon?
Are you the eyelashes or the dream?

Dai, dai, do, mm,
Dai, dai, do.
Dai, dai, do, mm,
Dai, dai, do.

Mm, mm, mm,mm.

Are you the flower or the nectar?
Are you the fruit or the sweetness?

Dai, dai, do,
Dai, dai, do.

Mm, mm, mm, mm,
Mm, mm, mm, mm,
Mm, mm.

SOUS LE CIEL DE PARIS*/ PISCINE MOLITOR PATEL**

*Written by JEAN DREJAC and HUBERT GIRAUD
**Written by MYCHAEL DANNA

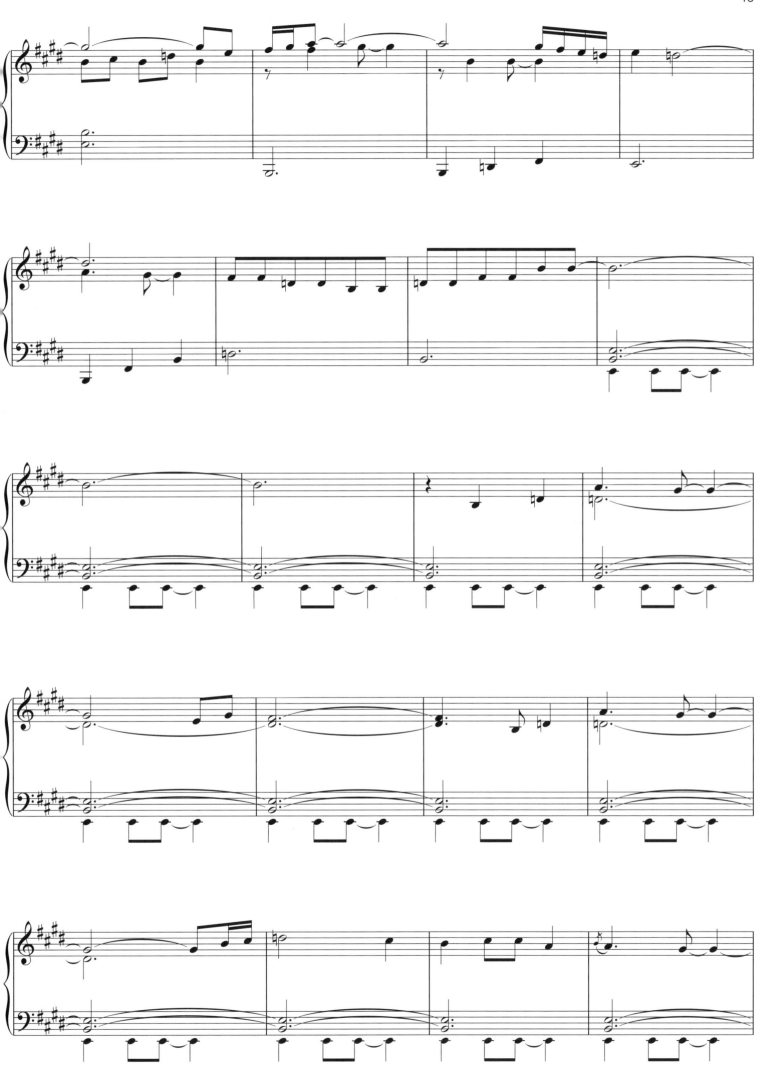

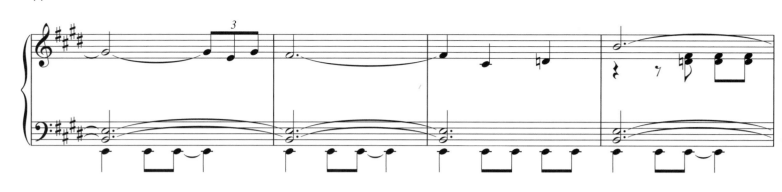

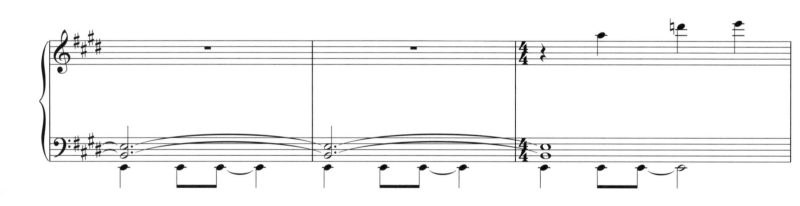

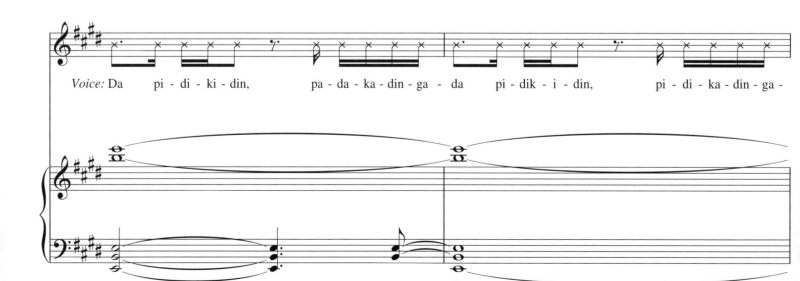

Voice: Da pi - di - ki - din, pa - da - ka - din - ga - da pi - dik - i - din, pi - di - ka - din - ga-

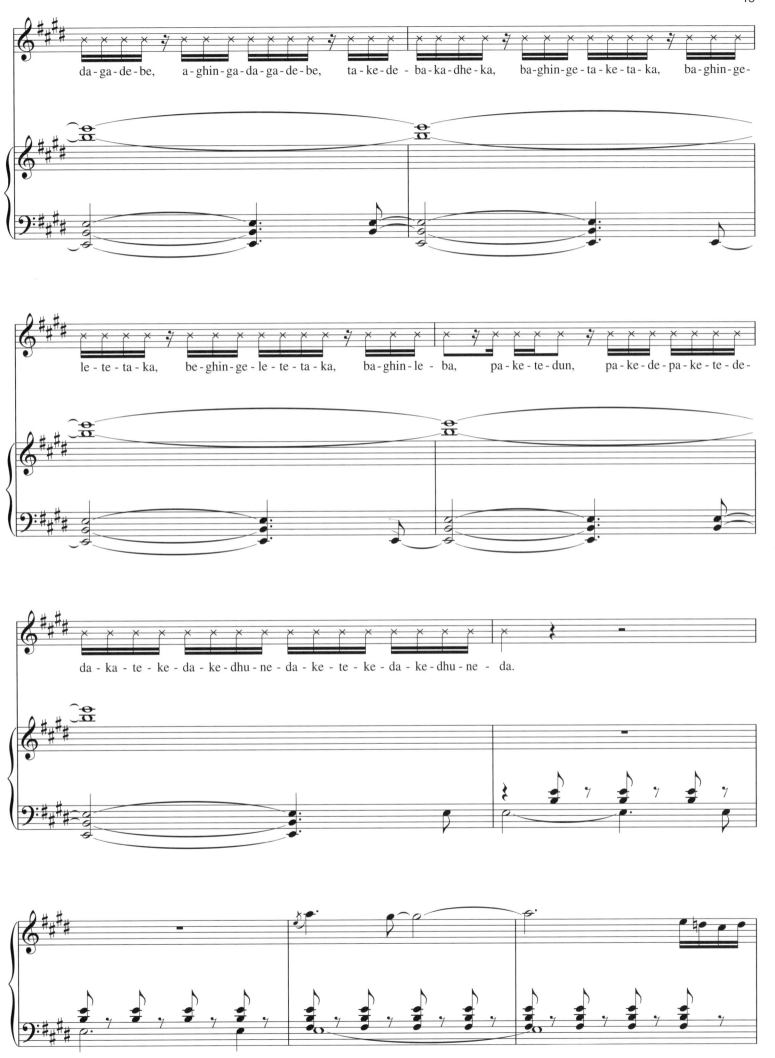

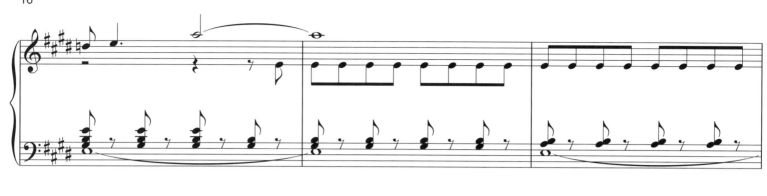

PONDICHERRY

Written by MYCHAEL DANNA

Moderately

APPA'S LESSON

Written by MYCHAEL DANNA

TSIMTSUM

Written by MYCHAEL DANNA

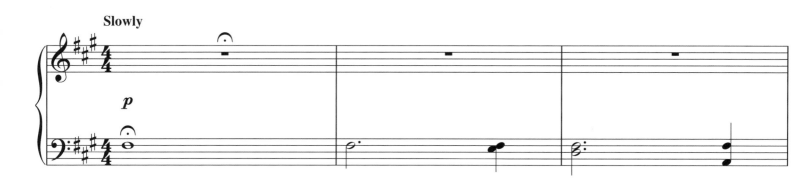

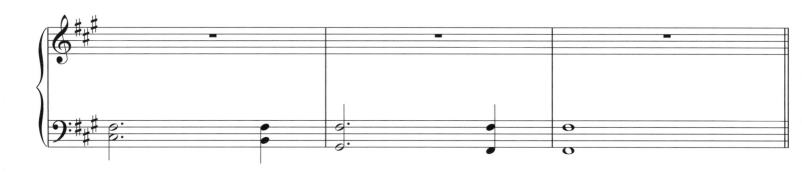

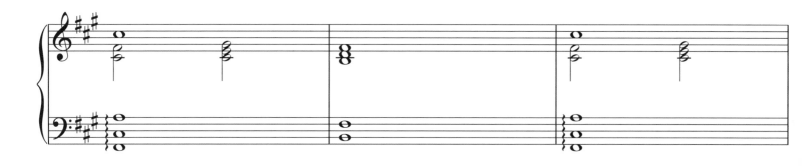

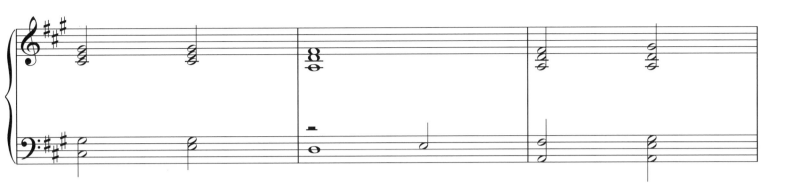

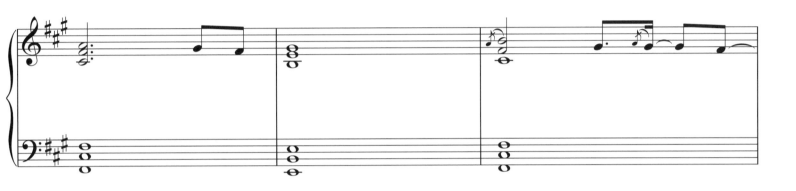

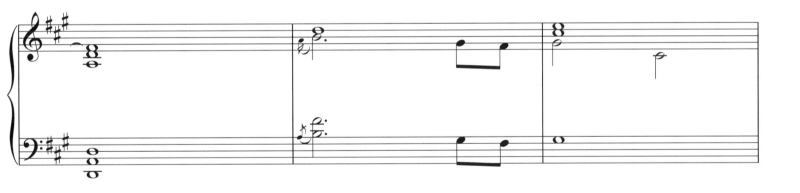

FIRST NIGHT, FIRST DAY

Written by MYCHAEL DANNA

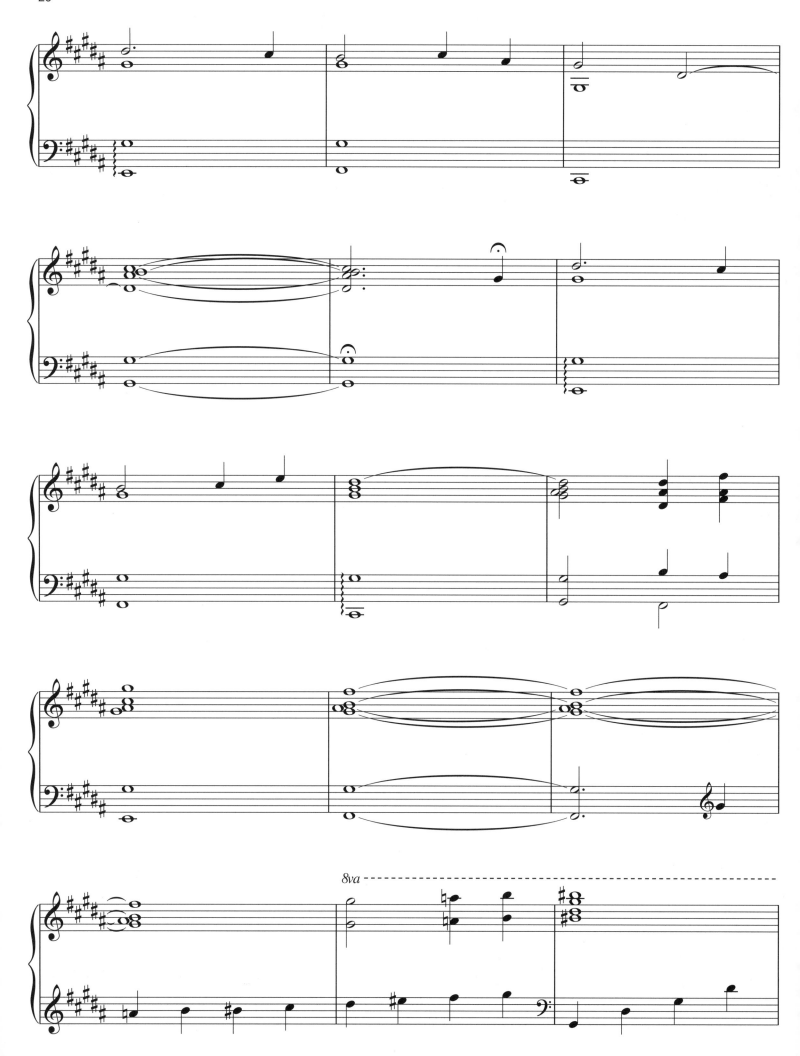

SKINNY VEGETARIAN BOY

Written by MYCHAEL DANNA

Moderately slow

PI AND RICHARD PARKER

Written by MYCHAEL DANNA

Moderately

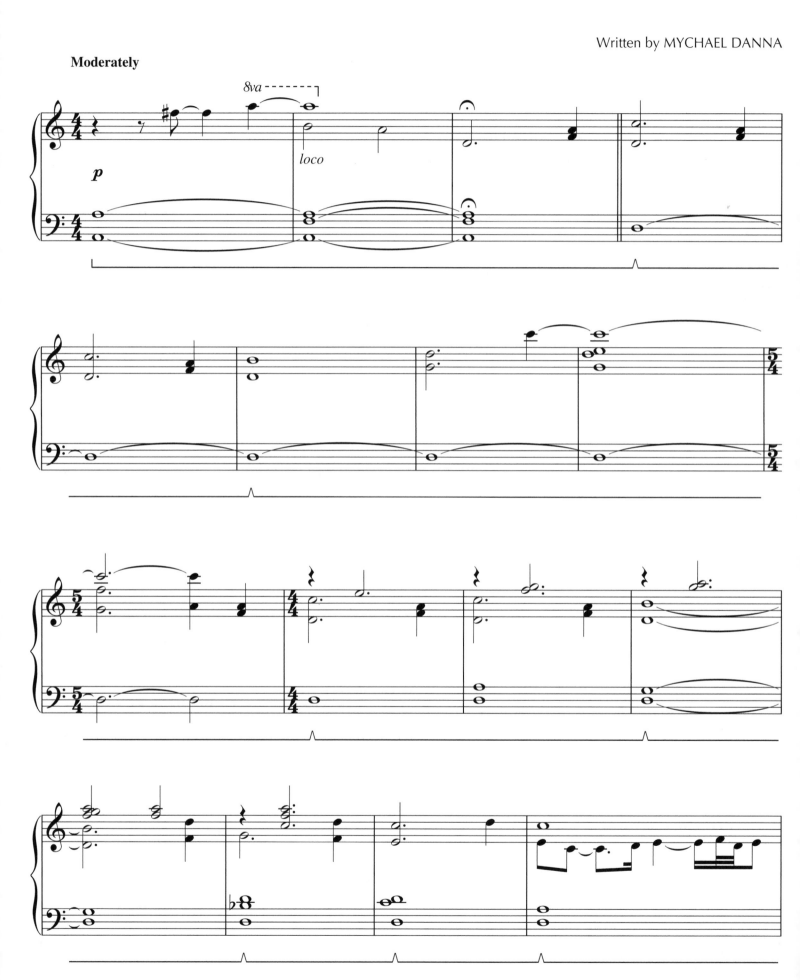

FLYING FISH

Written by MYCHAEL DANNA

Moderately fast, in 2

TIGER TRAINING

Written by MYCHAEL DANNA

Very slowly

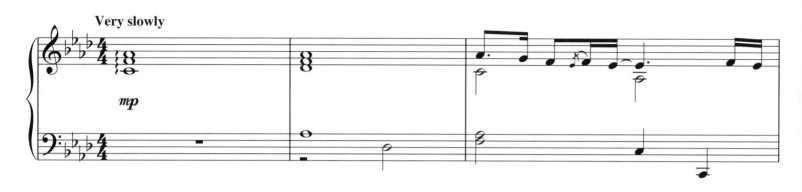

Moderately

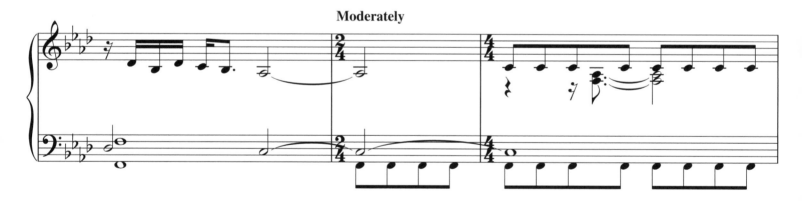

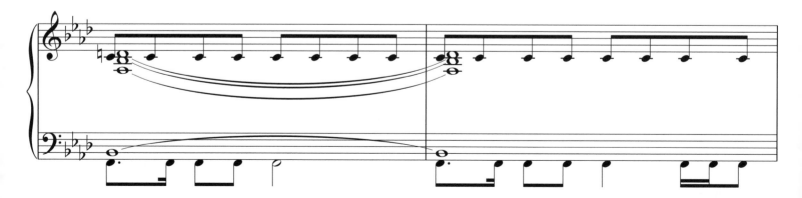

ORPHANS

Written by MYCHAEL DANNA

GOD STORM

Written by MYCHAEL DANNA

Slowly

Pedal ad lib. throughout

BACK TO THE WORLD

Written by MYCHAEL DANNA

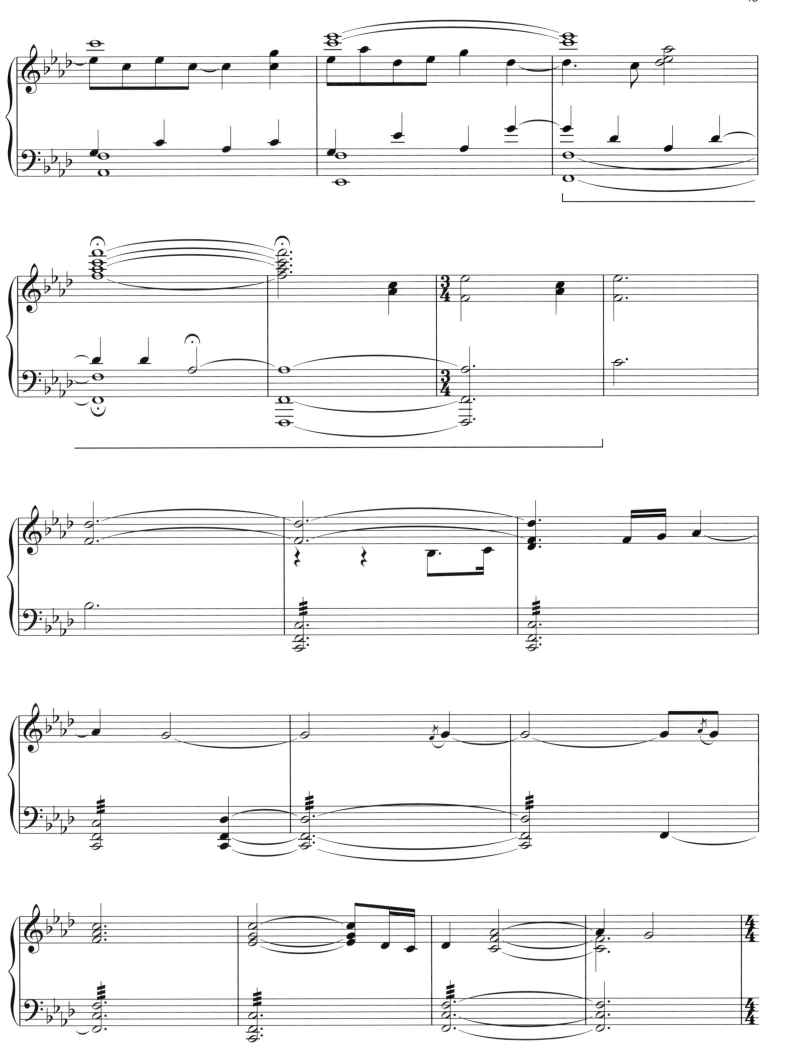

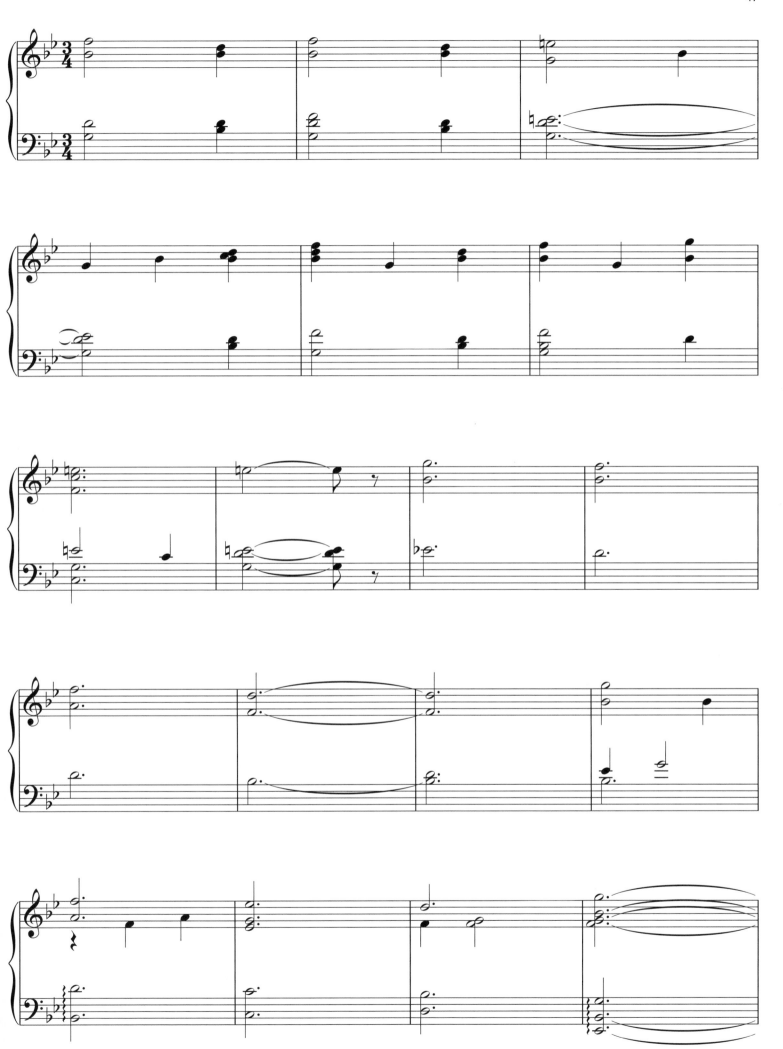

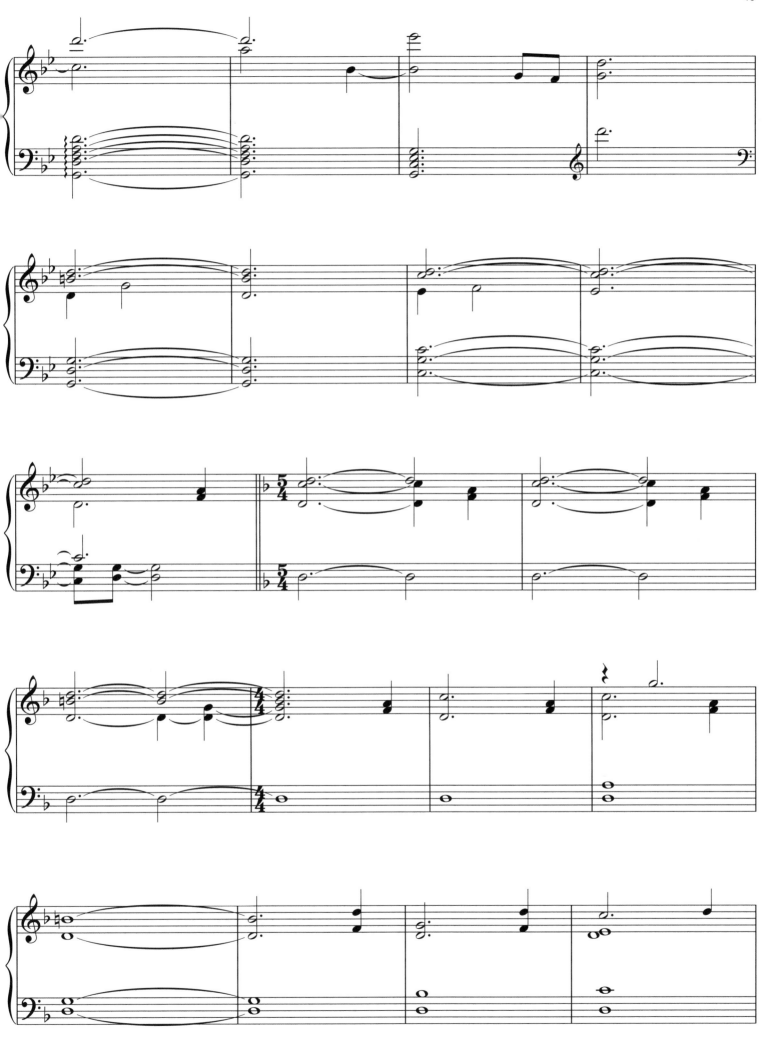

WHICH STORY DO YOU PREFER?

Written by MYCHAEL DANNA

Moderately

Pedal ad lib. throughout

THE ISLAND

Written by MYCHAEL DANNA
and ROB SIMONSEN